Maybe Swearing with Emojis will Help

Published in 2016 by
Nyx Spectrum

ISBN: 9780996764162

Printed in the United States of America

100% DONE WITH YOUR SHIT

I'm going to go stand outside. If anyone asks:

I'M HELLA OUTSTANDING

I

GIVE A

Mornings
Blow

DON'T LET MY FRENCH INTIMIDATE YOU.

THE OCEAN MADE ME SALTY

Made in the USA
Lexington, KY
02 March 2017